D1218849

Japanese Woodblock Prints

Japanese Woodblock
Their Techniques and Appreciation

by Umetaro Azechi

Published by
Toto Shuppan Company, Ltd., Tokyo, Japan
Japan Publications Trading Co., Ltd.
Tokyo, Japan   **Rutland, Vermont**

Prints

Foreword

The subject of this book is the making of Japanese woodblock prints. Japanese woodblock prints carry on the old tradition of the world-famous ukiyo-e, but the techniques for making modern woodblock prints are quite different from those of the earlier tradition. In this book, primary emphasis has been placed on modern print methods, and the discussion of appreciation omitted in favor of a later occasion.

Ukiyo-e was an art form expressed through the medium of printing, and the woodblock prints presented in this book are also the means through which art is expressed. The method is one of great freedom, and therein lies the excitement of woodblock prints.

Carving a block and printing from it with your own hands may seem rather difficult, but great skill is not so necessary. An unskilled person may, since the modern approach differs from the old in technique, produce works of unexpected interest and flavor. A print is by no means excellent just because it has been carved in detail; one sketchily carved may produce more satisfactory results. I think this will be better understood after reading this book, which has taken its print examples from works by artists who are still alive today, with the exceptions of Sempan Maekawa and Koshiro Onchi. The only work by an old master included in this book is that by Hokusai shown in Color Plate 1.

It will give me great pleasure if, by reading this book, interest is aroused in Japanese print techniques. I also hope that an understanding of the print-making process will further strengthen your appreciation for prints. To help increase this appreciation, I have included a section, Modern Japanese Prints and Their Techniques, with examples by modern print artists and explanations of their techniques.

Finally, I should like to express my warm thanks to the many print artists who readily contributed their works and to the Himawari Bijutsu Kai and the Nihon

Kyoiku Hanga Kyokai who contributed the children's
works for use in the figures and plates in this book.
I am also grateful to Mr. Charles A. Pomeroy for
translating the Japanese manuscript into English.

February, 1963

Umetaro Azechi

Table of Contents

List of Color Plates

List of Plates

Repose by Umetaro Azechi
This authentic woodblock print was designed and carved by Umetaro Azechi and hand-printed by Sokichi Kobayashi. The order in which the four colors were printed is blue, gray, red, and black (sectional method).

Color Plate 1   From 36 Views of Mt. Fuji, by Hokusai

A Look at Woodblock Prints

Whenever woodblock prints are mentioned, people are most likely to think of the Japanese ukiyo-e. Today, of course, ukiyo-e are highly valued as important works of art, but the wood block was originally employed as a printing technique without particular reference to artistic creation. The process is actually a simple one in which a deisgn is carved on a block of wood, ink applied to this, paper placed over it, and the back of the paper rubbed to make the print. It is by virtue of this very technical simplicity, however, that woodblock prints hold our interest, for they provide the means for a full display of artistic skill in the hands of the people who make them.

During the period when ukiyo-e were most actively produced in Japan—from the 17th century to the 19th century—a designer, a carver, and a printer co-operated in a division of labor to make woodblock prints. The famous Harunobu, Utamaro, Hokusai, and Hiroshige are among the great masters who painted original designs for prints during this period. At that time other printing techniques had not yet been developed, and woodblock printing was the only method used. It was also about this same time that the economy flourished and the culture of the common people reached its full flowering in Japan. This, in turn, brought about the practice of making many copies of one picture for the popular market. The woodblock prints of landscapes made in this period might be compared to the picture postcards of today, and the portraits to today's snapshot photographs. The development of a division of labor was for the purpose of mass production. That the products made by these artists and artisans through a division of labor remain today as precious works of art is decidedly an interesting phenomenon. In the final analysis it can be sad that this clearly indicates the value and interest of woodblock prints made by hand.

The early stages of woodblock printing techniques existed not only in Japan but also in other countries. Printing with wood blocks began in China about the 9th century and in Europe about the 14th or 15th century. In Japan woodblock printing was used many centuries before the era of the ukiyo-e. In recent times, however, printing techniques have progressed by leaps and bounds. One especially surprising thing is the influence of developments in photography on printing techniques. Such advances have made the woodblock printing industry of today an extremely small one.

Yet, woodblock printing differs from other types, and, as we have noted above, the woodblock print provides ample room for the artist to display his craftsmanship. Even splendid works of art can be produced, depending on the skill of the artist in giving life to the special expressiveness of pictures made by wood blocks. The development of the modern Japanese print was born of a viewpoint completely different from that of the printing craft. In contrast with their predecessors, who worked under the division-of-labor process, the modern woodblock-print artists came to do their own designing, carving, and printing. Also, in contrast with printing, the purpose was not to produce numbers of copies, so the artists were often satisfied to make only one print from a block. Such prints, made all around the world today, are called creative prints, and we make them because of our interest in them and our view of them as a handicraft as well as an art.

Anyone who first attempts to make a woodblock print will be surprised when he sees how completely the resulting picture differs from the design he has drawn. This is due to a special effect produced by idiosyncrasies in the wood block which makes the resulting picture different from others. For instance, a straight line cut directly with a chisel must certainly be different from one painted with a brush. Furthermore, the chisel differs from the brush in that very fine lines cannot be executed with it, so the woodblock print becomes a picture of concise expression by naturally omitting unnecessary details. Also, the pigments that are printed on paper after having first been applied to the block will carry different nuances than those that are painted directly on paper. When you sum up and estimate these effects and then find yourself inspired to try making woodblock prints, it will be because you have already entered deeply into the world of these prints. In fact, you may develop into a fine artist.

However, aside from this possibility for artistic

development, I think an attempt to make woodblock prints will be of great benefit to you personally for various reasons. This is because you yourself will draw the design, carve the block, and finally print it. In doing this, you will use various tools and materials, and your skill will be developed and polished. This, in turn, will enrich your life. If, for example, you can learn to make splendid woodcut Christmas cards to send to your friends, it will be a delightful achievement.

What is woodblock printing?

We have noted that printing with wood blocks is only one type of printing technique. There are, of course, various kinds of printing, and I think it is necessary for us to know what kind of printing can be accomplished with the wood blocks we are going to make. In the field of printing we have such general types as relief printing, intaglio printing, flat printing, and stencil printing (Figure 1). Let us take a brief look at each of these.

In relief printing, the part of the block face to be inked is raised. The ordinary movable print or phototype is like this.

Intaglio printing is just the opposite. For this, the engraved areas are inked, and the paper is pressed into them to make the print. The copper plate used in copper-plate engraving is of this type. When this is done on a large scale, it becomes gravure printing.

In flat printing, there is no surface unevenness, the face of the block is treated chemically, inked areas and ink-free areas are made, and the print is taken. Lithographic printing is of this type. The modern offset printing in wide use today is also of this flat type.

Stencil printing is the type in which perforations are made in the printing material and ink forced through them to make the printed form. Examples of this are the mimeograph, the stencil, and the silk-screen types.

Woodblock printing, then, belongs to the relief type. Accordingly, when a wood block is printed, the areas which appear as white will be those that have been carved out of the face of the block with a chisel. Furthermore, although this is true in all printing, the printed pictures or letters and the face of the block are reversed with regard to right and left. I think that seeing movable type has made

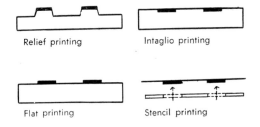

Relief printing   Intaglio printing

Flat printing   Stencil printing

1

Plate 1   Pond in a Park, by
            a school-boy
            (paper-block print)

everyone fully aware of this, but please call it to mind once more.

There is a kind of relief printing that can be done more simply than a woodcut. If a sheet of paper is presserd oved ink spilled on a desk, a pattern can be made from the irregularities and knots in the wood. This can be called the simplest form of relief printing, but it cannot yet be called a printing technique.

Paper-block prints

Here is a form of relief printing which, although simply done, produces a comparatively interesting effect. It is paper-block printing. To make a print of this type, cut the desired form out of stiff paper, paste it on a piece of cardboard of appropriate size, and apply ink to it with a mimeograph roller. When a sheet of paper is placed over this inked area and rubbed, the cut-out form will be printed on it. This is called a paperblock print, but it is printing by the relief method. Also, thread arranged in an interesting form on a paper block and pasted in place can produce a work that is not in the least bit foolish when it is printed. Plate 1 is an example of a paper-block print. In this picture the difference in height between the surface of the stiff paper and the base cardboard produces a white space around the stiff paper form, giving it an interesting picture.

I might add that there are also other relief-printing techniques which use such materials as kneaded clay instead of paper. However, we cannot call them advanced printings, and, when we compare them with woodcuts, the quality of the printing is inferior by far.

How to Make Woodblock Prints

Well, we are at last about to start making woodblock prints. First, the tools which must necessarily be provided are the woodblock chisels, a baren for use when printing, and a brush. In addition to these, pigments and a roller (to be used when oil paints are applied to the block) are needed. Before we set about making a print, however, the wood block, the chisels, and the baren must be eplained. These three are by all means the most essential and the most characterstic items used in making woodblock prints.

The block

What kinds of materials do we have for the block?

Wood blocks are of two types: those cut with the grain, called plank blocks, and those cut across the grain, called end-grain blocks. Figure 2a shows a section of an end-grain block in which the annual rings indicatng the age of the tree can be seen. The plank block is taken from a log in the same way as an ordinary board.

End-grain blocks are suitable for fine, close cutting, and detailed prints like phototypes can be made from them. Of course, the tools for cutting and printing are entirely different from those used for plank blocks. These blocks are also well suited to bear up under the pressure of printing, and large numbers of prints can be produced from them. Until the development of the phototype, end-grain block pictures were set with movable types and often used in such things as illustrated books. Unfortunately, since the wood is not cut length-wise in making end-grain blocks, large blocks cannot be made. If a large-size block is especially needed, the block face must be composed of several smaller blocks.

It is plank blocks, however, that have been used for the most part in Japan since ancient times (Figure 2b). The plank block is softer and easier to carve, and it is suitable for expressing the concise, bold, clear qualities of woodcuts. This type of block

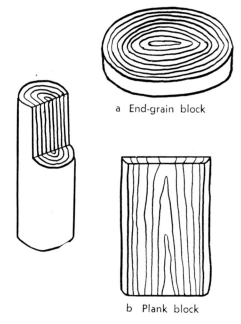

a End-grain block

b Plank block

2

is also easy to procure and can be obtained in large sizes — a feature that makes it suitable for large works. Since I consider the plank block more suitable for those unaccustomed to woodblock carving, this book will confine itself to explaining and describing prints made from this type of block.

Various kinds of wood are used for blocks. It seems that each country has found some particularly suitable wood to use, but any wood will do, so long as it is not too hard, too soft, too knotty, or too fine-grained. Generally, wood of the types noted below is used.

The Japanese ukiyo-e prints used cherrywood blocks. However, in addition to being hard, cherry is a high-grade and expensive material and thus not much used at present. Boxwood is also hard, and the end-grain block is often used, but, since there are no large trunks, it is difficult to make a large composition with boxwood blocks. In my opinion, the Japanese katsura (Judas tree) is the best for ordinary use. It is easy to carve, since it is not so hard, and it has few knots. Besides, it is easy to obtain. Wood from the ho tree is somewhat harder than katsura, but it too is easy to use. It is the wood least likely to warp.

Plywood is also suitable for wood blocks. It will not shrink or crack, it is somewhat softer than katsura, it is easy to carve, and pigments adhere to it well. Furthermore, it is cheap and can be obtained in large pieces, a factor which makes large-scale works more feasible. There are different types of plywood, but that made of shina is most frequently used. Since plywood is made of three or more thin sheets of wood glued together, the work of carving is made easier by simply peeling off the top layer of the cut-out areas.

Various other kinds of wood can also be used for blocks, such as jujube, shina, maple, and pear. Among other materials, linoleum is also useful. The surface is flat and of just the right hardness to permit the chisel to move easily and smoothly — a feature that makes it very easy to cut. One drawback, however, is the rubber-like surface, which makes it difficult to use liquid pigment when printing.

If the wood block is too thin, it will bend and may break during cutting; so it is desirable to have a minimum thickness of about one-half inch. If the block is three-fourths of an inch thick, it can be set

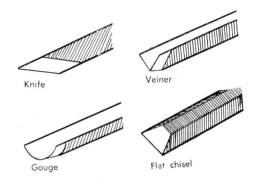

Knife   Veiner

Gouge   Flat chisel

3

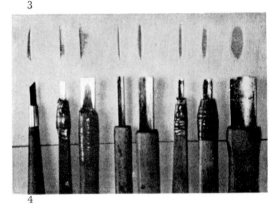

4

5

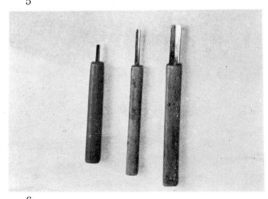

6

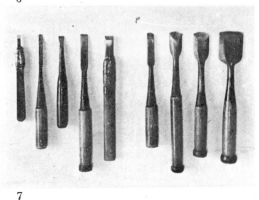

7

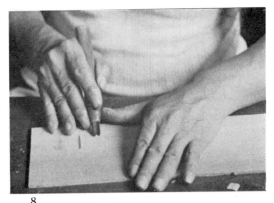

8

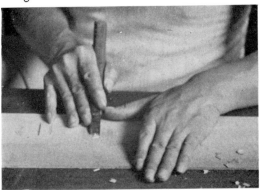

9

10

11

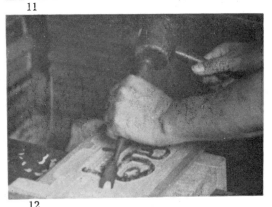

12

up on a printing press. Plywood is naturally thin, but that used by woodblock artists is about one-fourth of an inch thick. The wood block must be completely planed and then well sandpapered. This makes it much easier to print. Even if plywood is used, it is necessary to make the surface smooth.

The chisels

The chisels, as shown in Figure 3, are of four types. These four vary in size from large to small and are classified according to their uses, and are shown in Figure 4 together with the manner in which their cut lines appear in a print. They represent the minimum of tools required for carving, and are called the gouge, the veiner, the flat chisel, and the knife.

The gouge has a round blade, and the lines that it cuts have a soft nuance, since it produces a round groove in the block (Figure 5).

The veiner has an angular V-shaped point and makes a sharper incision than the round-tipped gouge (Figure 6).

The flat chisel has a wedge-shaped cutting edge like that of an ordinary chisel (Figure 7). It is used to shave out those parts of the block that will become the white areas of the picture. Also, since the lines made by the gouge and the veiner are straight and dull, the flat chisel is used to sculpture such lines as indentations (Figure 4 and Plate 9 on page 34). A further use for the flat chisel is that of removing the top layer of plywood after the lines have been made in it with the knife, as explained below.

The three tools just described are all used by being pressed forward (Figures 8, 9 and 10). The block, incidentally, is easier to handle if it is not too long. These three types of chisel are held in the right hand, and the fingers of the left hand are placed on the blade as shown in the figures. Lowering the wrist of the right hand and resting it and the little finger on the face of the block will give stability. To prevent the point from slipping sideways or cutting too much, place the thumb and the middle finger of the left hand on the blade as shown in the diagram. By laying the fingers of your left hand along the point in the way indicated in the figures, you will acquire a good "feeling" for making cuts from their reaction to the movement of the point. Accordingly, you will be able to make fine, dexterous finishes. Tools like the gouge, however, are also tapped with a mallet when cutting out broad areas as shown in Figures 11 and 12.

The knife is different from the three chisels just described, since it is used for the cutting of lines by being pulled towards the carver, as shown in Figures 13 and 14. Its use is very extensive, and it is an important tool that has been used since ancient times. When you are first cutting the block, pull the knife towards you while inclining it slightly towards the design line to make the outline of the picture. It might be said here that this cutting determines the final result of the picture. Since the knife has a quality of sharpness in its cutting, the picture will be vigorous when it is used freely (Plates 12 and 13 on page 37).

When removing the top layer of plywood with the flat chisel, as noted above, first cut a line vertically with the knife and then remove the wood with the flat chisel. This technique is not limited to plywood. After lines have been cut vertically with the knife in other types of blocks, the flat chisel is used to shave out areas which will appear white in the finished picture, making them stand out clearly.

Again, using the knife a second time, it is possible to make V-shaped cuts like those made with the veiner. These lines are different from those made by the veiner in that the slant of the cuts and their width can be varied. Please note and remember the differences between the cuts made by each tool, as shown in Figure 4.

Professional carvers not only cut towards themselves with the knife, but also use it by cutting away from them and to the right and left. Nevertheless, I think it is more usual and more effective to move the block in such a way that you can always cut towards yourself.

Care of chisels

The chisel must be sharpened if it does not cut cleanly. There are doubtless many ways to sharpen a chisel, and since everyone, I think, is fully aware of at least one of them, they will be omitted here.

When the cutting is finished, a light coat of oil should always be applied to the blades to prevent rusting. Vegetable oil is good for this purpose. Since the tip of the chisel will heat up when it is plied rapidly or worked heavily with a mallet, the tip should be momentarily placed in oil after use in order to cool it.

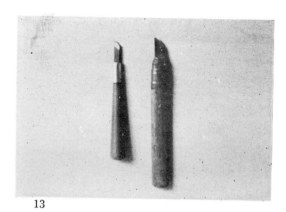

13

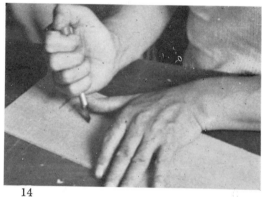

14

15

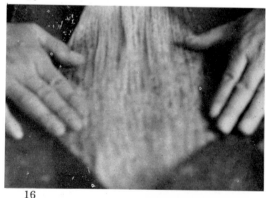

16

17

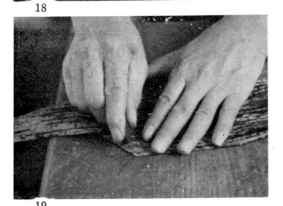

18

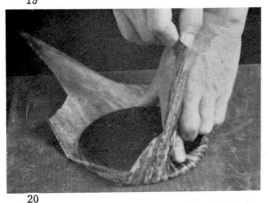

19

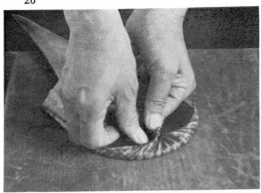

20

21

22

The baren

The baren is the implement used when pressing the paper against the block to obtain the woodblock picture. The baren seems to be best suited for plank blocks, and it has been used since olden times in Japan. It has also come to be widely used throughout the world in the making of woodblock prints.

The baren, as seen in Figure 15, is made of gathered threadlike materials wound in a spiral and fixed in a frame about 4 inches in diameter and covered with a bamboo sheath. The outside of the frame is painted with lacquer, but this is covered with several layers of Japanese paper called gampi. The wound spiral material inside the frame is bamboo sheath that has been finely split and then varnished with persimmon juice. This is the true baren. The lacquer and the persimmon juice are applied to make it waterproof, and the bamboo sheath itself is water-repellent. The bamboo sheath, the lacquer, and the persimmon juice are all traditional materials that carry the atmosphere of the Orient.

This baren made of bamboo fiber is the most suitable implement for applying pressure to the print, but it is difficult to make and requires much time and effort in the process. There are but a few craftsmen, even in present-day Japan, who know how to make a baren, so it is safe to refer to the process as a kind of handicraft art. Consequently, a true baren is very expensive, and substitute implements made from hemp or some other fiber are generally used.

Two wound spirals are shown in Figure 15. The one made of rougher material is used when pressing heavy areas, and the one of finer material is used when printing fine lines.

The bamboo sheath wrapped around the surface will become frayed after long use; so it must be re-wrapped occasionally. This operation is somewhat difficult, but a simple description is in order (Figures 16-25). Soak new bamboo sheaths in water until they are supple, then knead them with both hands to make them soft. When they are soft, spread them face down and, after removing the moisture, rub them well with some smooth object, such as the bottom of a bottle, to stretch them out. After making the ends the same width as the center, place the baren upside down on top of the bamboo sheath. If the sheath is too large, trim it to a suitable size and wrap the round container in it. Do this by first

23

wrapping up one side of the bamboo sheath tightly and, after finishing one side, wrap the other side, tying both ends tightly with string.

23

Do not forget to coat the face of the bamboo sheath on the finished baren with a little oil. The sheath will last longer if it is coated with oil after each printing.

The spiral filler inside the baren is rough but flexible, and the face of the bamboo sheath is hard, the fibers giving it just the right degree of roughness. When the prints are being made, this somehow naturally produces subtle nuances.

24

Bamboo, however, is not found the world over, and the wound material inside the baren is quite difficult for the ordinary man to make. Aside from the requirements of certain professionals, it is permissible, I think, for the ordinary person to make and use substitutes by himself. Various materials can be used, according to respective needs and plans. For example, such materials as cardboard or vinyl can be used as substitutes for the round container; rags can be used for the spiral packing; and some damp-proof material such as vinyl can be used for the face instead of the bamboo sheathing. These should meet the requirements for a baren, but you must be careful not to make it too large.

I think these various materials for a substitute baren are sold on the market.

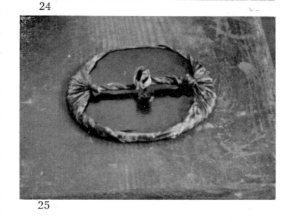

25

The old printers in Europe used rags wrapped in animal hide to make their prints. This implement was called a dabber. Also, it seems that they used a brush to press their prints, and this too may be a useful technique. Another device is to use the rounded part of a coffee cup — a suitable technique for prints pressed on an end-grain block but too smooth for plank-block prints.

Now we are finally ready to enter into the formal making of woodblock prints. First it is necessary to draw a design for the block.

Making the block design

In order to cut your block for the woodblock print, it is first necessary to draw the picture you are planning to print. There may be some original picture on which you wish to base your design. It may be a painting by some famous artist or a sketch made during your travels. Again, it may be a photograph or an illustration. However, if you do not have a

26

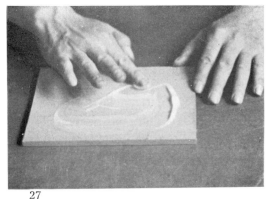

27

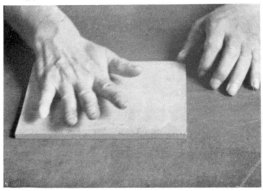

28

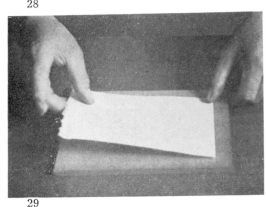

29

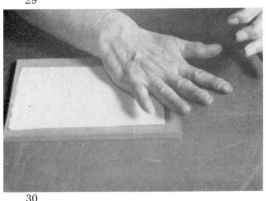

30

31

picture, it is quite all right to draw a design of your own inspiration.

Designs for woodblock prints are drawn on paper, but the paper should be semi-transparent and not too heavy. Anything may be drawn, and paint, crayon, or heavy pencil may be used. The ideal paper for this purpose is the Japanese paper called washi, which will be discussed later.

What kinds of designs are suitable for woodblock prints? This is a problem for your future consideration when you look at prints made by professionals and other artists, and we shall return to the subject again. For the present it is sufficient to say that designs which are too finely detailed are not suitable for wood blocks, for the lines are carved with chisels. Consequently, it is better to avoid minute lines as much as possible.

There is no reason to be disappointed about this. Professional print artists and people skilled with their fingers can make all kinds of fine lines, but when we draw our picture it is by no means necessary to include every little detail such as one would find in a photograph. What is most necessary, whether we do a portrait or a landscape, is to capture the essence of the subject and express it succinctly. I feel that even though our print designs are determined by the drawing and our chisels are restricted in use, we can master the essential points of artistic importance.

Also, there are some people who make a rough drawing of the design and then complete it when they carve the block. This procedure works well for the modern creative-print artists who carry out the designing, the cutting, and the printing of their own works. But since the cutting of the block is so important that woodblock prints are often called "knife pictures," the design procedure itself really makes no difference at all.

The techniques for drawing designs for the one-color (monochrome) print and the multicolor (polychrome) print are different, and the making of the difficult multicolor print will have to be explained later. In this book we first explain how to make a print from the design drawn for a one-color print.

Sometimes the design is drawn directly on the block itself rather than on paper. This is permissible, but, as we have noted earlier, the picture on the block must be literally the reverse of the finished picture itself. Thus, in this case, you must draw a reversed picture of the one you have in mind. If you are using a masterwork, a good design can be drawn in reverse by copying its reflection in a mirror. If you are not using a masterwork, your own design can be drawn on paper and then reflected in a mirror.

It is probably easier, however, to trace the design on the block from the paper than to draw it directly on the block. Most people do it this way, and there are two different techniques that can be used.

The first of these techniques is to smear paste over the face of the block, place the paper with the design drawn on it face down on the block, and then cut along the lines of the design that show through the back of the paper. For the design paper, as we have noted, it is necessary to use a semi-transparent paper that is not too heavy. It is easy enough to see why the paper is pasted face down on the block, for the block design must be the reverse of that which you desire in the finished picture.

Any kind of paste will do, but it is better to thin it, since it will be difficult to work with if it is too hard. When you apply the paste, it is first necessary to moisten the block with water and then to apply the paste evenly. After the paste has been applied evenly and completely over the block face, pat the entire surface of the block with the flat of your hand to make the work go more smoothly (Figures 26-28).

When pasting the paper, first paste the center to the block and then paste the rest of it carefully while spreading it toward the four corners with your fingers. The most important point is not to leave any wrinkles in the paper. If the design does not show through the back of the paper, a little oil should be applied to the indistinct areas to make the whole design visible.

Japanese print artists have for centuries used a special Japanese paper called washi for design paper. There are many different kinds of washi, and more will be said about this paper later, but any kind of washi will do for woodblock designs as long as it is not too heavy. Washi, in addition to being translucent, has very strong fibers which permit the removal of thin layers without tearing the paper.

The washi with the design drawn on it, as described above, is pasted upside down on the block (Figures 29-31). Then, before the paste completely dries, the rough fibers are gently removed by rubbing the back of the paper softly with the fingers, as shown in Figures 32-37. After the paper has been through-

32

33

34

35

36

37

38

39

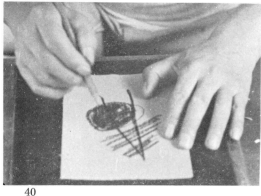

40

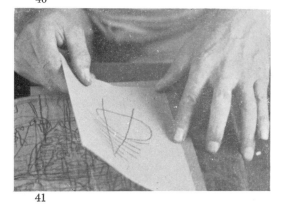

41

ly rubbed with the fingers in this way, it should be so thin that the remaining layer cannot be felt and the design appears to be drawn directly on the block (Figure 38). Figure 39 shows further corrections made on the block design with a pencil. Do this sort of thing freely and savor the interest of woodblocks. No matter how strong the washi is, however, be careful not to rub it too strenuously or the paper will tear.

Also, in the above method if the block design is drawn on paper that is too thin, there is a danger the paper will swell when applied to the block with paste. This makes little difference in the case of a monochrome block, but since a bad condition results when the paper swells it is probably better not to use thin paper in the case of a polychrome block.

This technique has been passed down in Japan from the old ukiyo-e period to the present. It was, no doubt, an especially necessary technique in the days of the ukiyo-e, when there was a division of labor among designer, carver, and printer, for the carver had to cut out the design faithfully, just as it was drawn. But since washi is indispensable for the employment of this method, it is impossible to use it in places where this paper is unobtainable.

The second technique of transferring the design to the block is to draw it on paper thin enough for it to show through—just as in the technique described above—then to place a piece of carbon paper face down on the block, place the design paper face down on the carbon, and trace the design on the block through the back of the paper with a graver or stylus, as shown in Figures 40-44. When the design and carbon paper are removed, the reversed design will be found traced on the block.

There is, however, one thing you must be careful of in using this method. Since the lines are traced with a pointed tool, they will be very thin, and this has to be corrected with a pencil in order to complete them (Figures 45 and 46). It may not be possible, in this case, to draw the lines exactly in the same way as they appear in the original design. The block with the most accurate design will by all means be the one made by the washi technique discussed above. But, unlike the artist of the old ukiyo-e period, the creative woodblock artist of today is not troubled by this. On the contrary, some present-day artists make only a rough outline on the block and then precisely delineate the picture as they carve it.

The design in this case is made without using paper. A general outline can be made by painting the design with an oil-base paint on glass, placing the painted design face down on the block before it dries, and then rubbing the glass to make the design stick to the block. This will give you a reversed outline of your design, and the block design can be perfected with a brush if you wish to do so. Glass is not the only material that can be used for this method, for any stiff paper that will not absorb the pigment can be used.

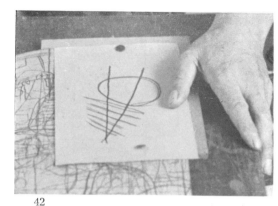

42

The easiest and most convenient method to use, however, is the one that employs carbon paper, as described above. Consequently, it is better to use this method in making your first woodblock design.

When the block design is finished, paint the entire surface of the block with a very thin coat of black ink—so thin that it will not obliterate the design. The purpose of this is to make the carved areas of the block stand out clearly so that none of the places to be carved will be missed.

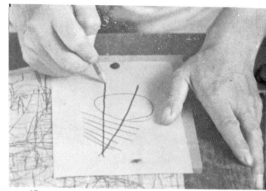

43

Carving the block

Carving begins after the block design is finished. The block is carved following the lines of the design, and this carving is the most important part in making a woodblock print. It is so important that we can say the quality of the print is for the most part decided by the carving. It is for this reason that woodblock prints are called "knife pictures." With this in mind when you are carving, use the chisels with the intention of making vigorous cuts and without being too fastidious about details. Remember that the world of those who "paint" with a knife is a different world.

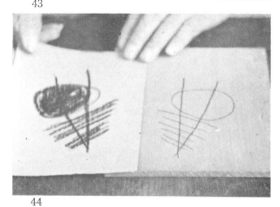

44

The four types of chisels—the gouge, the veiner, the flat chisel, and the knife—and the ways of using them have already been described. Please call their uses to mind once again. If you understand how to use the chisels, we can begin carving, but keep in mind that wood blocks are cut in relief, as explained earlier.

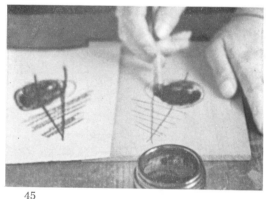

45

For example, in carving one line the area around that line is carved out to leave the line raised. Thus, when the block is inked, the lines will become black and the surrounding areas will be white. This is called positive carving (Plate 2). However, if a block with the design traced on it is given to someone, like

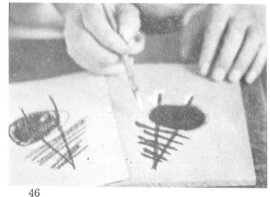

46

Plate 2   Temple Pagoda, by a school-boy
(positive-print technique)

Plate 3   Fire-cracker, by a school-girl
(positive-print technique)

a child, who knows nothing about woodblock prints, he will reverse the process and carve out the lines. When such a block is printed, the lines will appear as white, for the black and the white are reversed. This, however, is not necessarily wrong. It is a method that is intentionally used to get a certain pictorial effect and is especially suitable for depicting night scenery. Indeed, it is a very simple technique, which makes it suitable for beginners. This technique is called negative carving (Plate 3). Most woodblock prints are executed in the positive carving technique, but the negative carving technique is also quite interesting (Color Plate 9 on page 101).

Moreover, the use of the positive and the negative carving techniques together in one woodblock print often occurs (Plate 4). When this technique is skillfully used in making black-and-white prints, it tends to impart complex nuances to otherwise dull and monotonous prints. When a detailed carving technique is used, this method can be employed to make realistic prints that closely represent the natural appearance of things (Plate 5). Examples of such fine prints can be seen in Europe and modern China. In opposition to this type there is a technique that strives to make a strong contrast between black and white by adding the intermediate tones to one extreme or the other. The prints in Plates 6 and 7 are of this type. A vigorous impression will be

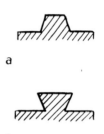

a

b

47

48

49

Plate 4

People on a Pier, by a school-boy (combination of positive and negative techniques)

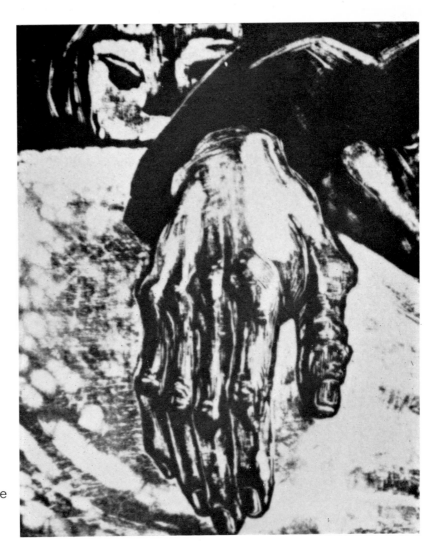

Plate 5

Composition (portion), by Makoto Ueno

(Combination of positive and negative techniques, sketchy line technique)

50

produced by using a strong carving technique (Plate 36 on Page 89).

At this point I shall make an attempt to explain the main points and the small details to be aware of when carving the block. Keep them well in mind and apply them when you are carving.

Two examples of carving techniques are shown in Figure 47: the correct method in a and the incorrect in b. If all carving were done as in a, it would be ideal. This is especially true in the case of plywood carving, as described earlier. If the lines are cut at an angle with the knife as in a, the top layer can be removed easily, but this will be somewhat more difficult if it is cut as in b. There is also the danger that the block will break.

Not only plywood but the wood of any block design will crack during printing if the carving is done as shown in Figure 47b. On the contrary, if the block is carved as shown in a, the raised surface will only become wider when many prints are taken and the surface is worn down, so that if the design is recarved the block can be used again. If it is carved as shown in b, this will not be possible.

Plate 6   Child with a Toothache, by a school-girl
(contrast of black and white)

Plate 7   Visiting an Aquarium, by a school-boy
(contrast of black and white)

51

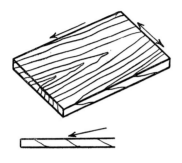

52

53

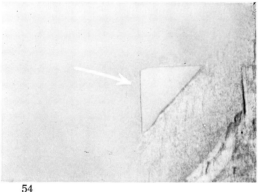

54

55

Again, the carving of the lines should first be done with the knife in such a way that the raised surface of the block is beveled in forming the cut lines. This determines the general outline of the block. Then, taking the situation of the design into consideration, you should carve out the block by using the flat chisel, the gouge, or whatever else is required (Figures 48, 49 and 50). However, the carving need not necessarily be done this way. Carving the entire block by using only the gouge and the veiner will produce an interesting work uniform in aspect (Figure 51, Plate 8). The block print in Plate 9 was carved using only the flat chisel. A notched line is carved by the flat chisel. This permits us to refer once more to woodblock prints as "knife pictures." There is much freedom in the use of the chisels.

Of course you are well aware that wood has grain. The block must always be carved with the grain, as shown in Figure 52. It is difficult to carve when you come up against the grain, but this difficulty can be overcome by changing the position of the block and by using the tool at an angle against the grain of the wood.

The block must always be carved with moderation. Avoid overcutting, for excessive cutting will make the finished picture hard and lifeless. This is particularly true in the case of black-and-white prints (Figure 53). It is probably better for the inexperienced printmaker to carve only a little at first, to make trial prints, and then to carve out additional areas wherever he thinks it is necessary.

It is permissible to insert a wooden plug when excessive cuts or mistakes are made. This sometimes produces interesting results, especially when a plug of a different type of wood, harder or with a different grain, is used. Technically, inserting a plug in an ordinary wood block is rather difficult, but in the case of plywood the construction of the material offers an advantage in that a wooden piece can be glued into the area where the top layer has been removed. Taking this into consideration, you can see that it is better not to carve any deeper than the first layer in plywood. Figures 54 and 55 show a plywood block with a plug and its printed result.

Ink will naturally seep into the broad sections carved out of the block, and the paper will take this ink in printing if it is pressed down into these depressions. If this is the printer's intention, it will

Plate 8   Deity, by Yoshio Kanamori
(use of gouge and veiner only)

Plate 9
Face, by Tomio Kinoshita
(use of flat chisel only)

Plate 10   Mt. Yatsu, by Susumu Yamaguchi
(block gradation technique)

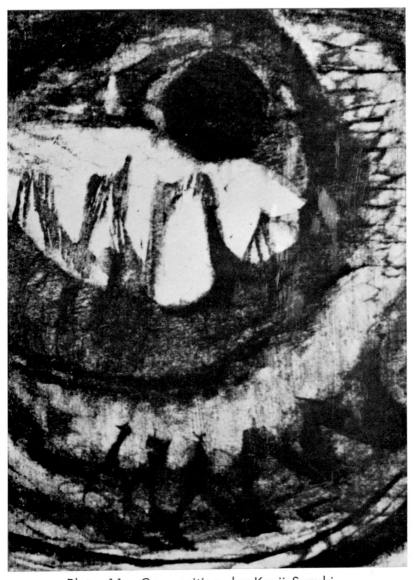

Plate 11   Composition, by Kanji Suzuki
(block gradation technique)

make little difference, but if it is not his intention, it will be better to carve out deep drains for the broad areas and shallow drains for the narrow areas.

There is a technique called block gradation. This is the gradual thinning of the block as shown in Plates 10 and 11. In cutting the lines to produce this effect in the carved block, the knife is first used to make flat angles and then the flat chisel is used to make gentle slopes. In printing, the ink or the pigments will gradually "take" more strongly toward the upper part of the slope and thus produce the effect of gradation.

It should be kept in mind that the carved lines will be distinct to the degree that the knife is applied in nearly vertical cutting (Figure 56 and Plate 12). Furthermore, the design will be very tight, especially in prints where the knife has been used freely to cut the block (Plate 13). An interesting picture like that in Plate 14 can be made by using the knife freely.

The next point is probably well known, but it should be noted here. Usually the design is carved in the center of the block in such a way as to leave a surrounding border. If this is done, it is easier to make the print, but this border should appear as a white edge when printed, so it must be cut lower than the surface of the block with the gouge or the flat chisel (Figure 57).

It is important to shake out all of the shavings after the carving is finished. Then you must check to make sure that no part of the carving has been overlooked. It was for this purpose that the block design was covered with a thin coat of black ink. Nevertheless, effective results are sometimes gained from carving misses resulting from carelessness (Figure 58). This happens because the form of a miscarving or a miss that is naturally made may unexpectedly break up the monotony of a picture. There are even some print artists who purposely make calculations to obtain this effect (Plates 15 and 16).

There is a problem involved in the hairlike wooden fuzz left on the carved lines. This should be removed with a chisel, no matter how fine it may be. Avoid plucking it off with your fingers. Since wood has a grain, careless plucking will pull up long slivers and spoil the lines that have been carved with such difficulty.

If the design paper was pasted to the block, remove the remaining paper with a damp cloth,

56

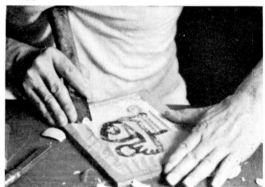

57

58

59

Plate 12   Doubtful Flower, by Shiro
Takagi
(effect of vertical cutting)

Plate 13   Melancholy, by Tamami
Shima
(effect of vertical cutting)

Plate 14   Arabesque Woman, by Takuya Tamamura
(effect from free use of knife)

Plate 15   Fish, by Sho Kidokoro
(miscarving used for effect)

Plate 16   Voyage of a Fish, by Hiromu Sato
(miscarving used for effect)

taking special care to remove the paste along with the paper.

For your final reference, Figure 59 shows a finished block.

The carving stand

A certain amount of strength is used when carving a block with chisels. For this reason, it will be convenient to make a carving stand to prevent the block from slipping during the process. If this is not done, the process will be somewhat laborious. Professional printmakers have carving benches to make their work easier, but the ordinary person does not require such elaborate equipment. Any type of stand can be devised according to the individual printmaker's inclinations, but the following recommendations should be sufficient.

Lay out a board about 1 foot wide and 16 inches long and nail a narrow piece about 1/5 inch thick to the left edge. If the block is placed against this edge, even when such chisels as the gouge are tapped with a mallet, the block can be managed without its slipping. But, since the stand itself may move at times, a similar narrow piece of wood should be nailed to the underside of the opposite edge of the stand. The carving base can be used without its shifting when this piece on the bottom right side is fitted against the side or front edge of the work table, as shown in Figures 60 and 61. Since this simple base is sufficient, it should by all means be used.

Printing the woodblock picture

Since woodblock prints are made by relief printing, the pigment or ink is applied to the raised surface and the paper pressed against this. That is to say, pigments or ink and the means for applying them to the block, tools for pressing the paper against the block for printing, and finally the paper itself are needed. These items will be discussed before we explain the printing techniques.

The pigments

Both water-base pigments and oil-base pigments are used in printing. Among the water-base pigments we have India ink, poster colors, water colors, and pigments for Japanese-style painting. Since poster colors fade, they are not too well suited for artistic

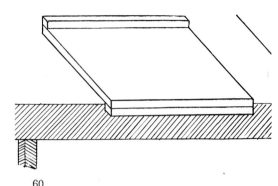

60

61

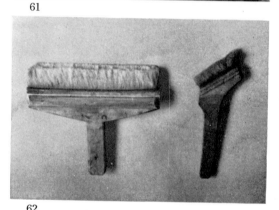

62

63

64

65

66

67

68

69

appreciation, but they are convenient for simple quantity production. Generally, water-base pigments are soft and settled in feeling after they have been printed. Japanese printmakers have used these pigments for centuries. But they dry out easily and may therefore be difficult to use in the drier areas of the world. Also, they are not very good for printing on soft, absorbent paper. This point will be explained later.

Among oil-base pigments we have such materials as oil paints, mimeograph ink, and ink used in flat printing. Oil-paint colors are very beautiful, but there is danger that the oil contained in them will saturate the paper during printing. To prevent this, it is better to squeeze out the quantity to be used onto absorbent paper several hours beforehand in order to permit the excess oil to be absorbed. Also, after this oil paint has been printed and the print has dried, it is best to back the print with another sheet of paper, for a print without this backing will decompose in time. Mimeograph ink can also be used, but since it too will saturate the paper, it should be prepared in the same way that oil paints are prepared.

The ink used in flat printing, such as lithograph and offset printing, is hard and cannot be used as it is, so it must be softened with a few drops of turpentine or kerosene while it is being worked with a spatula. It has a beautiful color and will not leave oil stains, but the finished print will have a bright sheen, and the color nuance is not so good as that of oil paints.

Oil pigments are suitable for dry climates, since they dry slowly. On the other hand, this slowness in drying makes the work difficult. It makes no difference which kind of paper is used for printing. For the most part, the result of printing oil-base pigments is clear expression of the line design and fine variations on the surface of the block. But since oilstains occur easily, it is better to avoid designs with broad light areas.

The brush and the roller

The brush is used when applying water-base pigments to the block surface (Figures 62 and 63). The orthodox brush is made of horsehair, but since this is a little too stiff, professionals soften it before they use it. One method for this is shown in Figures 64-66. First, the tip of the brush is singed in the flame of a candle then rubbed on the abrasive surface of dried shark skin (an ordinary file may be used). When this is done the bristle tips split and become finer, making it more convenient for applying pigments.

In using the brush, first soak it in water and then shake out the excess water to leave the brush in a slightly moistened condition. Next, dip the brush into the container holding the pigment in order to charge it, and then apply the pigment to the block. Figures 67-75 show pigments for Japanese-style painting being thinned with water and applied to the block. In some cases the pigment comes in tubes. Since one side of the brush will wear down if it is always moved in the same way, it is better to move the brush uniformly from side to side throughout the operation. The brush must be thoroughly washed after use.

As a substitute for the orthodox brush, a shoe-brush, a paintbrush, or a toothbrush can be used. The shoebrush or toothbrush should have fine bristles and should not be too stiff.

A roller similar to that used in mimeographing will be fine, and a small roller is preferred to a large one. The roller is used for applying oil-base pigments to the block. In using such pigments, place the paint on a pane of glass or a palette and spread it with a spatula. After a thin layer has been spread out, the roller should be moved over it in such a way that it will be coated uniformly. The roller is then rolled over the block to apply the pigment. Figures 76-83 show oil-base pigments being used with a roller and applied to a block. First, squeeze out the oil color on a glass plate, place a newspaper over it for two or three hours, and after the oiliness has been removed use the roller. Paint remaining on the roller after it has been used must be removed with soap and water.

The paper

It is necessary to take the pigments into consideration in deciding what paper will be used for printing.

Oil-base pigments can be printed on any paper, but hard-finish paper is not suitable for multicolor prints because the pigments lie on the paper without being absorbed. In this connection it seems that Japanese washi or Western newsprint is the best for printing. Moreover, as will be explained in more

70

71

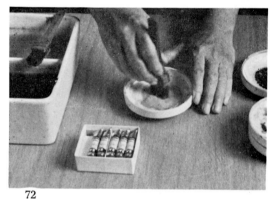

72

73

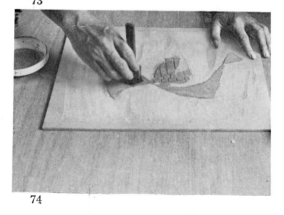

74

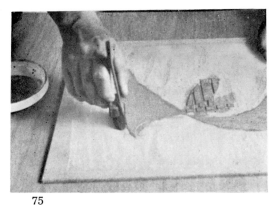

75

76

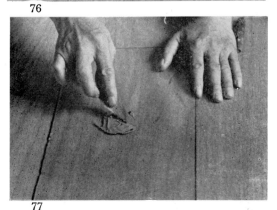

77

78

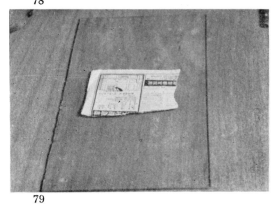

79

details when we consider the water-base pigments, the paper should be dampened before printing to soften the fibers and make it more pliable for easier printing. But too much water is not good, since oil and water are mutually repellent.

Water-base pigments are difficult to print. When they are applied to dry paper, the moisture in the pigments causes swelling that results in wrinkles in those areas of the paper where the pigments are printed. Furthermore, water-base pigments will blot when printed on paper that is too soft and absorbent. For this reason, the paper must be prepared and printed in one operation.

Dry paper must be slightly dampened before printing. There are many ways of doing this, but something on the order of an atomizer that can be used to coat the paper with a mist is sufficient. Of course, more water is used for heavy paper and less for light paper in moistening. The paper to be dampened can be moistened easily by placing it on a square of vinyl or some other waterproof material, from all four corners, and allowing it to stand for 20 or 30 minutes (Figures 83-90). The moistened paper will take the pigments better and will not wrinkle, as noted above. Also, since the paper will be softer, the pressure applied to the baren will be more effective.

There is, however, some difficulty in the case of multicolor printing. This is due simply to the fact that the paper will dry out during the time-consuming process of printing many colors. One method of counteracting this is to wrap the paper in another piece of waterproof material after each printing of a color. Another method is to place the paper between two sheets of moistened blotting paper after printing each color.

This technique of using blotting paper can also be employed in moistening the paper for the first time. Dampen the blotting paper with a brush and place the sheets of paper to be moistened on top of it. Then cover these with another sheet of wet blotting paper and let the stack of paper stand overnight. Stack the sheets at a ratio of about ten of printing paper to one of blotting paper. It will be better in most cases, if three sheets of blotting paper are used together at the top and botom instead of just one. If parts of the paper dry out during the process of printing, you should dampen only those areas by using an atomizer.

Pigments tend to blot when water colors are used on soft paper, especially the soft Japanese washi. To prevent this, a substance called size is applied to the washi. Sized paper can be found on the market, but since unsized paper is more common, it will probably be better for you to do the sizing yourself.

Size is made by mixing glue and alum with water that has been brought to the boiling point. The approximate measurements should be one liter (slightly over one quart) of water, about 1½ ounces of glue, and a pinch of burnt alum. This should be suitable, but it is better to make the liquid thin rather than thick. If the size mixture is too thin, then two coats should be applied. As you undoubtedly know, glue must not be placed directly over a fire, but should be mixed with water — about one glass for the amount given above — and dissolved over a low flame. After the glue has been dissolved, it should be mixed with the hot water in the proportion given above. The burnt alum is added to the mixture after it has been dissolved in a little of the hot water placed in a cup. This size mixture should then be filtered through a cloth and thoroughly applied to the paper with a brush before it cools. The paper should then be dried. The size will seep in between the fibers of the paper and fix it in such a manner as to prevent blotting.

In drying the sized paper each sheet must be dried separately, for if the sheets are stacked they will stick together. A convenient way to dry them is to string a wire across a room and hang them up (Figure 91). Also, the brush used to apply the size should be washed thoroughly after use. If this is not done, the bristles will stick together and make the brush useless.

This type of size is used not only for woodblock prints, but also for painting with water colors on washi or on silk—in each case to prevent blotting. But size has another use in each case to prevent blotting. When it is applied to soft, flimsy paper, it serves to prevent the paper from sticking to the block and also assures that the paper will be pressed firmly against the block during printing.

It seems that water-base pigments are somewhat difficult to use, but when prints are made with these pigments on washi, a paper that takes the pigments well, deep and serene colors are obtained. This permits the creation of compositions with nuances

80

81

82

83

84

85

86

87

88

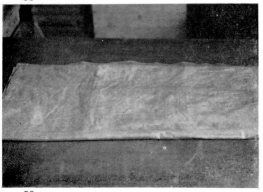

89

that are difficult to describe. Recall, for example, the flavor of Japan's old ukiyo-e prints. The excellence of Japanese woodblock prints derives to a great extent from this wedding of water colors and washi. Every beginning printmaker should by all means try this technique. We shall have more to say about washi later on.

Preparations for printing

The pigments, their application to the block with brush or roller, and the paper used for woodblock prints have all been described above. With this preparatory knowledge stored away in your mind, you can now apply the pigments to the block you have carved and print it by yourself. The baren and the other tools used in printing have already been explained. Printing, of course, is the final step in the creation of the woodblock print, but no matter how skillfully the printing is done, if the carving on the block is bad, a good print cannot be produced. The carving, in the end, is the most important element. I think you will feel this much more keenly after you start your own printing.

Now, before you start to make your first print, it is necessary to arrange the required tools and materials around you to make your work easier. What shall we prepare? You probably know from the explanations given up to this point, but it is a good idea to recall them.

First, there are the pigments. If water colors are used, you will need dishes to put them in, as well as a brush. If oil-base pigments are to be used, you must have a pane of glass or a palette to spread them on, a spatula, and a roller. Then you must have the baren for printing and such items as clean rags and oil. It is also necessary to have utensils for washing the brush and the roller. In addition, it is a good idea to fix the block so it won't move. Two or three wet towels placed under it will take care of this; even small wet pieces of cloth placed under the four corners will do. You must also place a piece of vinyl material or oilcloth under the block to keep the table or bench clean. It is often necessary, too, to have a wiping cloth. Make your preparations without forgetting anything.

The printing process

The main points and details calling for attention during printing will now be explained.

The techniques for applying pigments to a wood block have been described earlier, but a few more points will be brought out here. With water-base pigments, the colors will adhere better to the paper if very small amounts of thin paste are dripped here and there on the surface of the block before applying the pigments with a brush. Also, since the face of the block will not take the pigments well when it is dry, you should first wipe it with a damp cloth or a brush for water colors or with an oily cloth for oil colors. Be careful not to let the pigments plug up the drains in the block.

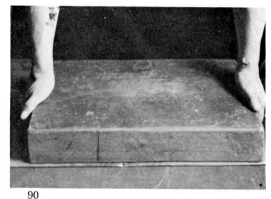

90

The paper is placed on the block after the pigments have been applied. If only one color is used, the paper is generally placed on the block from the center out. We have noted earlier that a border should be left around the block when it is carved. If the paper is cut to the size of the block and the corners of the paper are matched up with those of the block, the picture will be in the center. (This must be done more accurately when you are printing several colors, and the technique for doing this will be explained later on.) After the paper is in place, rub it lightly toward the four corners with the baren to stretch it and make it stick tightly to the block (Figures 92-94). If this is not done, the paper will slip, and the result will be a double image. Also, care should be taken that no air remains between the paper and the surface of the block.

91

When you use the baren, it should be held as shown in Figure 95 and pressed around and around to make the paper take the print. Before you do this, however, you should apply a very small amount of oil to the part of the baren that comes into contact with the paper. Do not rub too hard at first, but after once more stroking the entire surface lightly, you can rub it in a more ordinary way. If this is not done, it is possible that either the bamboo facing on the baren or the paper itself will tear on the rough edges of the shavings left in the hollowed-out parts of the block. Tearing can also be caused by hard bits of pulp that are occasionally present in the paper. Finally, keep well in mind the condition of the surface of the block when you are applying the baren. It is foolish to use unnecessary strength in trying to press the paper into the carved-out areas.

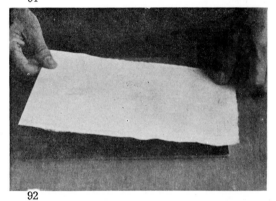

92

The strength with which the baren is applied differs according to the condition of the pigments

93

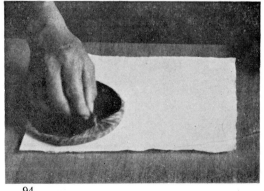

94

95

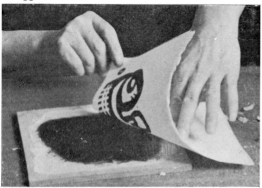

96

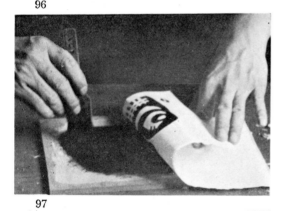

97

98

99

and the condition of the block surface. It is necessary to press down rather hard in taking color from the wide areas of the raised surface, but not so much strength is applied to the narrow areas. If the pigment is applied lightly and the paper pressed hard, a direct, sharp impression like that in Plates 17, 18, 19, and Color Plate 3 (page 52) will result. An oil pigment was used in Plate 18. Accordingly, the effect is somewhat different from that of the water colors used in Plates 17 and 19. Conversely, a heavy feeling like that conveyed in Plates 20, 21, and Color Plate 2 will result when much pigment is applied and the paper pressed lightly. Furthermore, depending upon how the baren is used, various subtle changes can be produced by the way pressure is applied. You will understand this better as your experience accumulates. When you feel this at first hand while you are printing, it will, I think, give you a greater appreciation of the value of the baren.

When the paper is pressed on the block after moistening, or when the pigments blot through to the back, there may be some difficulty in rubbing it directly with the baren. To overcome this, another sheet of paper with a slick surface should be placed on top of it and rubbed.

The condition of the pigments should be inspected at least once during the process of printing. You must remember, however, that when the paper has once been removed from the block and the print found to be in bad condition, it cannot be replaced on the block as it was before. An attempt to do so will result in the printing of a double image. The correct method for making the inspection is shown in Figure 96-99. One side of the paper should be held down with the hand or a weight and the other side gently pulled up for a look at the print.

If the color is too thin, try pressing down on paper a little harder. If the color still does not take well, then the pigment must be touched up. Blotting of the color indicates that too much pigment has been applied to the block, or that possibly too much water was used in moistening the paper. If the examined side of the print seems to be all right, however, inspect the other side in the same way and proceed with the printing.

In the case of postcards or other cards done on stiff paper, you will have a different problem, since the sides cannot be lifted up for inspection. For

Plate 17   Composition, by Rikio Takahashi
(thin water pigment and hard pressure used)

Plate 18   Waning Moon, by Kunihiro Amano
(thin oil pigment and hard pressure used)

Plate 19   Concern, by Toshi Yoshida
(thin water pigment and hard pressure used)

Plate 20

Composition with a Red Ball,
by Chizuko Yoshida
(thick pigment and light pressure
used)

Plate 21 Noodle Boy, by Yoshitaka
Nakao
(thick pigment and light
pressure used)

Color Plate 2. Rush, by Rokushu Mizufune
(thick pigment and light pressure used)

Color Plate 3   Impression of a Garden, by Ansei Uchima
(thin pigment and hard pressure used)

printing of this type, a registry mark, called kento in Japanese, is made on the block in order to fix the position of the paper and is used to match the paper to the block in its original printing position after it has once been removed and inspected. This registry mark will be discussed below in connection with multicolor printing.

When a test print has been made and its condition is unsatisfactory, no matter what you have done, additional carving of the block will be necessary. We have noted, in regard to the areas to be carved, that only a little carving should be done at first. Blocks that have been overcarved cannot be corrected. We have also mentioned the insertion of a wooden plug by way of correction, but is not successful every time it is attempted. Also, the technique is rather dfficult, except in the case of plywood. The technique of undercarving at first is much to be preferred.

Another point to take into account concerns fine lines. When such lines are carved somewhat lower than the face of the block and the paper is pressed lightly over them, sketchy lines and a hatched surface can be produced, as shown in Plates 5 and 22.

Gradations, as we have noted before, are another aspect of printing. When gentle slopes have been carved on the block, the pigments will gradually coat the lower areas of the block during printing, and gradations will result. It is also possible to produce gradations by printing techniques alone—that is, without the use of carving techniques.

There are many methods. There is shading done by charging the brush with water, dipping the tip in a pigment, applying it in a straight line on the block, and then laying the paper on the block from the top with the baren. There is shading done by wetting the block well, applying heavy pigments to it, wiping the edges with a damp cloth, and then printing. There is shading done by wetting the block with a brush, applying pigment over it many times with another brush to naturally shade the one side.

There are a variety of methods like those above, but they were all used in the old ukiyo-e period for such things as the sky gradations of Hokusai and Hiroshige (Color Plate 1) However, block shading is the most used today, for the effects are more certain. Yet, the following method is also used today, and I think it is interesting.

Plate 22   Stone Garden at Ryoan-ji Temple, by Masao Maeda
(sketchy line effect)

Plate 23   Camellia, by Kaoru Kono
(old style shading)

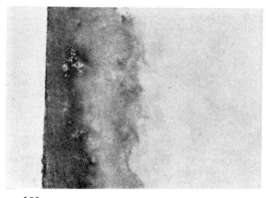

100

First, amply moisten the block, apply the pigments, and place the dampened paper over it, then rub it with the baren. The pigments spread through the water on the block and an unexpected natural effect appears (Figure 100). But this only works well when the pigments are of a water base type. Plate 23 shows an interesting use of the old style shading. The white area in the center was roughly shaved with a chisel like the veiner, the pigment applied and wiped lightly with a cloth, then printed.

Occasionally you will find that the block warps slightly during printing. When this happens, dampen the bottom of the block, and it will return to its original shape.

Multicolor printing

Up to this point, we have been dealing with the making of one-color or black-and-white prints. But most of the prints that we all see at exhibitions or hanging on the walls of people's homes are beautifully colored. Black-and-white prints are very fine, but prints done in a variety of colors are even finer, and everyone, I think, who has gained experience with one-color prints must feel a desire to try his hand at making multicolor prints. Nevertheless, it is unreasonable to try to make a complex, many-colored print at the beginning, so it is better to start with something like the simple color prints shown in Figure 105 (page 59) and Color Plate 9 (page 101).

Actually, of course, there are two colors even in black-and-white prints, since they use India ink, which is capable of gradations. Differing from works of a solitary color, these prints can produce an atmosphere of light and shade and a complexity of expression, as shown, for example, in Plate 24.

However, when you are making a tinted print in two colors (or more), the paper, which is printed on two blocks (or more), must have its position well defined or it is likely to be misprinted, as can be readily seen from looking at the print shown in Figure 105. This picture is a simple two-color woodblock print, but if the positioning of the eye in the picture were even a little bit off, it would look extremely odd. For this reason, the position of the paper when it is placed on the block is very important in multicolor printing, and it is for this purpose that the registry marks are used.

Plate 24   Birds and Mountain, by Umetaro Azechi
("two color" black-and-white print)

The registry marks or kento

The marks used in determining the position of the
paper on the block are called registry marks or kento.
These marks are shown in Figure 88.   Usually each
block used in making a print has a "key" mark, made
in the shape of an L, in the lower lefthand corner, and
a straight-line mark at the lower right hand corner.
These together form the kento. .We have noted
earlier that in carving the block the central area is
carved and the margin shaved, so that when the
finished print is removed there will be a white border
around it.   When you shave this border out of the
block, the knife or the flat chisel should be used in
such a way as to leave these two marks at the lower
left and the lower right corner (Figures 101 and 102).

These marks should be indicated on the block
design for each color to be printed.   Accurate registry
marks cannot be made if this is not done.   As each
block is printed, the position of the paper must be
determined by matching it perfectly to the marks:
first the lower right corner to the 'key" mark and then
the lower left edge to the straight line (Figure 103).

101

102

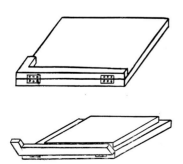

103

104

Nowadays there is a device that is widely used instead of registry marks — that is, a registry piece. You can make this quite easily yourself by affixing an L-shaped piece of wood to the edge of a board with hinges, as shown in Figure 104. You can immediately see that this will become a mark for determining the position of the paper. The block is placed on this board and fitted snugly into the L-shaped mark, and when the paper is placed on the block, it is in turn fitted snugly to the registry piece. After the position of the paper has been determined, the hinges are used to drop the registry piece, and then the paper is printed. Of course, the registry piece must be of greater thickness than the block.

It is necessary, in using such registry pieces, that the carving be done after each design has been drawn in a fixed position on paper of a fixed size and that the design paper be pasted to each block in a fixed position. Conversely, the registry piece can also be used in determining the position of the design for each color and the position in which the design paper is to be pasted on the block.

Making separate color blocks

There are two methods for making a separate block for each color; the key-block method and the sectional method.

In the key-block method a black-and-white block is made according to the original design. This is used as the basis for making each separate color block, a process which is shown in Figure 106 (page 60). The black-and-white block is fitted to the registry marks, and several prints are made (Figure 106). Then, following the original design, one color is applied to a print. First, green has been used in the illustration.

Using this as the block design, the printmaker then carves out all but the area to be printed in green, thus making a block for that color (Figure b). The registry marks must be matched up with a print from the black-and-white block. In the same way, a third block for the grey and a fourth for the red are carved (Figures c and d), and when a print is taken from each of these blocks in b, c, d and a sequence, the result will be like that shown in Figures b, e, f, and g. This finishes the process.

But perhaps your print doesn't seem to be quite right. Is this possibly because your first black-and-white print is too strong? When you follow the above method, there is a tendency for this to happen. If you feel that this is the case, carve out the areas of the key block that you think are unnecessary (Figure h) and print each block in succession once more. The result will be similar to that shown in Figure i. When you compare it with the result shown in Figure g, you will see that it looks much more attractive.

The sectional method uses a technique in which the block design for each color is taken directly from the original design or the original picture. In most pictures there is something like a key block that provides general unity, but when this is missing and many colors are simply merged together, there is no general basis for determining the key. The sectional method is probably the only one that can be used in a case like this.

Figure 107 (page 62) shows a polychrome print made by this method. Place a thin sheet of paper over the painting and draw first only the grey areas of the design (Figure a). In this case it is necessary to make registry marks on the picture and match it with the block design paper. Use this for making the grey color block. Next, make blocks for each of the other colors in the same way, such as for brown, red, and black (Figures b, e, and d). Registry marks, of course, are made on each block. When a single sheet of paper is printed consecutively on each color block (Figures a, e, and f), the finished print will be like the one shown in Figure g, which was printed by this method. It was completed by superimposing the four colors from a, b, c and d of the figure on the paper.

Color Plate 4 shows a print made by the key-block method and Color Plate 5 by the sectional method (pages 64 and 65).

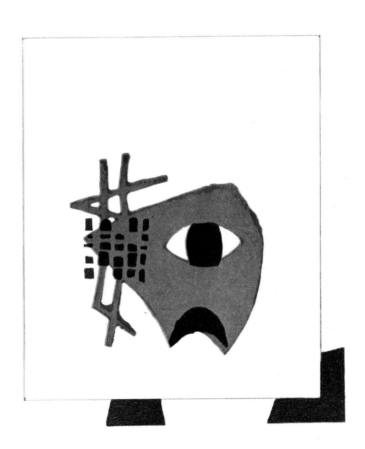

a

b

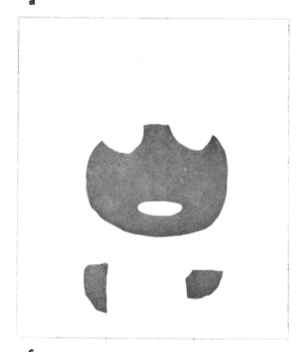

c

d

e

f

g

h

i

61

a

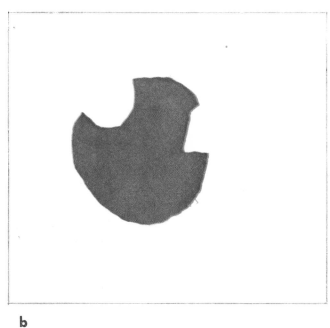

b

c

d

e

f

g

Color Plate 4   Ancient Korean Capital, by Un'ichi Hiratsuka
(key-block method)

Color Plate 5   Pond, by Hide Kawanishi
(sectional method)

108 Combination of three primary colors (page 67)

109 Colors superimposed and printed with wood blocks (page 67)

Each color is numbered to indicate the painting sequence.

Some precautions in multicolor printing

There are a few points in the making of multicolor prints upon which care must be exercised. These are discussed below.

When you are printing with wood blocks, the combining of pigments will not produce results like those obtained when pigments are mixed in the usual way. Everyone knows the three primary colors well and that blue combined with yellow produces green, that red combined with blue produces purple, and so forth (Figure 108 on page 66). But this is not true when you are making woodblock prints. If yellow is printed over blue, for example, it will not result in green, but only a bluish yellow will be produced. This is also true when blue is applied over red, for the result will only be a reddish blue. There is no remedy for this, since there is no way in which the three primary colors can be combined in woodblock printing by merely printing one color over another.

Figure 109 shows the conditions when colors are mixed by superimposing them with blocks, in which a is applied in a red, yellow, and blue sequence, and b in a yellow, red, and blue sequence. Notice the difference between this and the three primary color combinations in Figure 108. The combination of colors by woodblock is varied by such things as the manner in which pigments are applied and the manner in which the baren is used in printing. This is fully learned through experience.

There is a printing technique for primary colors called heliotype. In this, fine-meshed plates are used to print patterns of dots in each primary color, and when these are printed together, a variety of colors can be produced. But a wood block is no more than a flat board, so it cannot be employed in this fashion.

Still, this does not mean that colors can never be combined, for they are often superimposed in woodblock prints. There is, however, no principle for primary colors. By doing a lot of multicolor printing and including the results of your experience in your calculations, you will come to learn the conditions under which colors can be combined in woodblock prints.

Another point to note is that it is not always necessary to use a separate block for each color. Depending on the nature of the picture, colors that are seen in the distance can be printed from one block. Since this is a very important factor in the efficient printing of multicolor prints, learn it well and put it into practice.

The sequence in which the colors are printed will probably be different for each design. The black-ink block was once the first to be printed, but today it seems to be printed last in most cases. This is because it gives the picture greater strength. Figure 106 is printed in this way. Also, when a dark color is printed first and an opaque light color printed later, a feeling of volume will be produced. Experience and study will further enrich your knowledge of this use of color.

We have mentioned this earlier, but after your first print has been completed you will no doubt be surprised when you see how different it is in expression from the block design you first drew. On inspecting the print, you will make various discoveries, such as disappointing spots that were unforeseen and places that produced unexpected results. But it should be remembered that there is a sharp difference between a picture executed with a brush or with crayon and one executed with a chisel or a knife and colored through the medium of a wood block.

Let's look at the finished print once more. The unsatisfactory places may be due to inexperience with woodblock techniques or to the unsuitability of the picture for woodblock printing. If, in your next attempt, the whole picture or even a part of it seems unsuitable for the woodblock technique, it should be dropped. Grasp well the point that unexpected results often appear, and try to make use of this fact in a practical way.

Furthermore, it is important to use the woodblock prints of others as references. The successes and failures of other printmakers are important to you. By learning from them, you will more quickly enter the world of woodblock prints.

Quantity production of woodblock prints

How many prints can be made from one block? The modern creative print artists by no means aim at quantity production, but this problem will probably be of interest to you.

End-grain blocks are made from hardwood and cut in such a way that a fine grain is produced. This permits them to print sheets running into the thousands. In fact, so many prints can be taken from them that they are often set up together with movable type. Still, plank-cut blocks should not be considered lightly in this respect. As many as two or three thousand prints can be taken from one plank-cut block, although the hardness of the wood plays an important part in this. In this connection, cherrywood blocks are quite good, but ho and katsura are by no means inferior when it comes to quantity production, if they have been treated correctly and care is taken in the carving and the printing. One thing that requires attention is the slanting of the base of the raised surfaces when the block is carved. As we have noted earlier, if this is done properly the block can be recarved and used again after a number of printings have worn down the raised surface.

As another means of increasing the durability of the block, professionals usually soften the stiff brush used to apply the pigments during the printing process. But you can help to increase the durability of the block even without doing this. Merely be careful not to apply the brush strongly to the edges of the raised surfaces. The same precaution applies when you are using the baren. The surface irregularities of the block must be thoroughly understood, and care must be taken not to apply too much pressure to the edges of the raised surfaces.

You will find it possible to turn out a large number of prints from a single block if you pay attention to these details and print with care.

Special printing techniques

There are quite a few different printing techniques that have been used from times in the distant past. There are also techniques that have been devised in recent times. These may be difficult for those who have not yet acquired a large amount of woodblock printing experience, but they will be explained below for your reference.

One of these techniques is that of mica printing. Instead of pigments, glue is applied to the block where desired and then printed on the paper. Mica dust is applied to the paper before the glue dries. Once it dries, the excess dust is removed. The semitransparent mica dust adhering to the glue has a glitter (from its mineral source) that changes with the angles of view and produces an interesting effect. Utamaro and Sharaku both used ths technique for backgrounds in their portrait works. Gloiopeltis paste can be melted and used instead of glue. This technique is not limited to mica dust. Luxurious prints can be made if gold dust or some similar substance is used.

Blank-impression printing is another of these special techniques. If segments of the block are left unpigmented, irregular impressions of the carved lines can be produced by rubbing the baren over them. These lines are perfectly visible in the print, even though no color appears (Figure 110). Rather interesting nuances can be achieved when the technique is used skillfully.

There are also prints that are made completely without color. To achieve such a print, place a sheet of paper on the unpigmented block and rub it with the baren. Since a gloss will appear on the areas of the paper that are pressed and an irregular surface is formed, an interesting picture results. In Japan, these are often used for such things as candy boxes. In Plate 25 a press was used to produce an especially strong effect in a colorless print.

110

In still another special technique the grain of a wood block can be used to produce some unsual forms. If the grain is left as it is, an effect can be achieved by applying pigments to it and then making prints (Plates 26 and 27). In recent years the fine grain of plywood has often been used for this purpose. One technique is to print the same block twice, once lengthwise and once crosswise, to produce a netlike effect, as shown in Plate 28.

The block used in Plate 29 is plywood, but the mesh effect in the lower center of this picture was not made by wood grain. Instead, canvass was stretched over the block, pigments applied, and the print made. It often happens that effects are produced without cutting by using various materials when printing.

When a wood block is carved shallowly, making an engraving, and pigments are applied to the carved-out areas, the baren can be rubbed over it lightly to give you a color print that is soft and light in appearance. This technique makes the original relief-type woodblock print into an engraving.

The negative-print technique, which consists of carving the line area in reverse, as described in the section on carving, can also be used (Figure 111). Here, white or some light color is printed on black paper, so that the black areas of the paper become

111

Plate 25 Forbidden Play, by Jun'ichiro Sekino
(colorless print)

Plate 26   Composition, by Reika Iwami
(utilization of wood grain)

Plate 27   Street by Day, by Toshiro Maeda
(utilization ot wood grain)

Plate 28 'May Rain, by Fumiaki Fukita
(utilization of plywood grain)

Plate 29   Birth, by Goro Kumagai
(canvas used in part)

Plate 30   Rain, by Tadashige Ono
(negative-print technique)

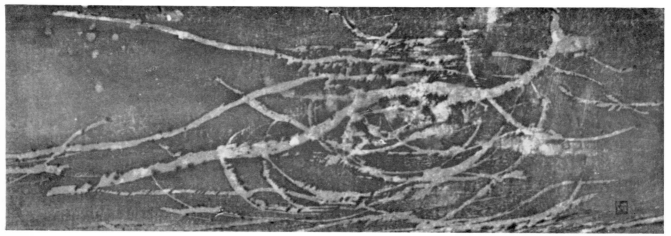

Plate 31   Violence, by Joichi Hoshi
(negative-print technique)

Color Plate 6   Composition, by Hiroyuki Tajima
(negative-print technique)

lines (Plate 30). Instead of black paper, apply the ground color to the uncarved block and print the desired number of sheets. It is interesting to print in the negative technique on these colored sheets (Plate 31, Color Plate 6 on Page 75).

The pigments must be applied rather heavily in this case, or the technique will not work. Excellent decorative works can be made on heavy, thick paper, depending on such things as the color of the paper and the color of the pigment used in printing. It might be interesting for you to try a picture like the konji kindei (gold dust on dark-blue) background), a type that has been made in the Orient since ancient times. The use of gold dust has been explained above in the paragraph on mica printing.

There is also a technique for printing the back of the paper, so that when the print is viewed from the front the color shows through thinly, like shading. When this is matched up with a print on the other side of the paper, a three-dimensional feeling is given to the picture (Plate 40 on page 97).

One more technique is the one known in Japan as kappa-zuri—that is, stenciling. This is the same as mimeograph printing, and it is also used together with the woodblock technique for producing multi-color prints. As in the key-block method of color printing, the outline is first printed in black, and each color is then painted separately on this. Next, a backing is made from some heavy paper such as drawing paper, and then the areas to be colored are out. This is called a pattern. Place this pattern on a print from the black-ink block and then apply each color separately with a brush. Only the areas that have been cut away are painted. In this way many colors can be applied, but water colors should be used for best results. Also, since this is a form of multicolor printing, it is necessary to determine the registry marks for each color, as we have noted earlier. It is interesting to note, with regard to this method of printing, that among the famous origami (paper folding) papers of Japan there is a beautifully patterned one called chiyogami that has always been made by the kappa-zuri technique.

Finally, I should like to touch on rubbing or 'impression' printing. This printing technique has been used often since olden times. It differs from the woodblock printing method, and when this method is attempted on a woodblock the results are quite

112

113

114

115

116

Plate 32   Deity, by Kihei Sasajima
("rubbing" made with inked pad)

Plate 33   Delusion, by Kazumi Amano
("rubbing" made with crayon)

interesting. Paper is placed on a carved block and tapped lightly with an inked pad of rolled cloth (Figures 112-118 and Plate 32). The ink may be of either an oil or water base.

Instead of ink, materials such as crayons may be used to rub the surface. This will make the finer areas stand out more clearly (Plate 33).

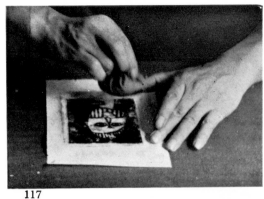

117

118

A note on Japanese washi

The term washi has been used many times up to this point in our discussion of woodblock printing. Washi is a special paper that has existed in Japan since ancient times, and Japanese woodblock prints, from the days of the old ukiyo-e to the present, have generally been made on this paper. In fact, washi has been used to such an extent that Japanese prints cannot be thought of apart from it. Since its fibers are tough and difficult to tear, it was used in old Japan for cloth. At one time the paper was hand-made sheet by sheet. Even today, high-grade washi is still made completely by hand, and the value of the paper is decreased if it is not hand-made. In washi the fibers of the paper mulberry are well entangled and do not have a grain like that found in Western paper. No less importantly, washi is very pliant and absorbent.

There are various kinds of washi, but in general they are all beautiful to look at, and when it comes to the high-grade washi made by hand, all of it is so fine that it is like a work of art. Described briefly below are some of the types of washi together with their uses in the making of woodblock prints.

The paper called hosho was used in old ceremonies, while nishinouchi and minogami were named after the places where they were produced. These types are thin but strong. Minogami is especially suitable for making block designs. The paper called torinoko (literally "chicks") is so named because it was originally of an egg color. Today much of this torinoko is bleached white. It is a heavy paper, its production process is advanced, and it has a wide market. The hosho type called masa (hosho-no-masa) is produced in the greatest quantity today, and when someone speaks of hosho in general, he is speaking of this paper.

In addition to the nishinouchi mentioned above, the torinoko and the hosho-no-masa types are probably the best for woodblock printing. All of these types, of course, are absorbent, and since water colors used on them will blot, they must be sized by the process that we have described in an earlier section. Some hosho-no-masa paper is sized and some torinoko is made non-absorbent in the manufacturing process, and these should be easily obtainable, since they are widely exported by Japan. These are convenient papers to use.

In addition, shoji paper—the paper used in Japan for sliding doors and windows—can be used for small prints. There is also the heavy kyokushi paper, which can be used for a variety of purposes.

Samples of washi

hosho

nishinouchi

minogami

torinoko

(hosho-no-masa)

The washi samples were made by the Fukui Shigyo
Co., Ltd., Tokyo, Japan.

Modern Japanese Prints
and Their Techniques

Color Plate 7
Space by Masaji Yoshida
Using only a gouge, the interesting composition
after carving and the extremely clean printing have
been preserved.
(Size: 115″×115″)

Color Plate 8

Ballad by Gen Yamaguchi

This work preserves the techniques of printing. The background is printed in a thinned water color. The round area in the center does not looked carved, and in this case a round piece of paper was placed on the inked block when printed.

(Size: 158″×232″)

Plate 34
Girl Selling Flowers in Kyoto by Sempan Maekawa
The lines are carved mainly with a knife.   A little ink
and light pressure on the baren were used in printing.
(Size: 62″ × 94″)

Plate 35

Lyric by Koshiro Onchi

Printed with well thinned water colors. There is no shading. The white lines in the center were made by pasting some material like string or tape to the block to prevent the pigment from touching the paper in this print. It is not carved.

Plate 36
Two of the Great Ten Disciples of Buddha by Shiko
Munakata
The lines were all carved with a knife, giving them
great strength.   Note well the contrast of black and
white from the use of positive and negative carving.
(Size: 38″ × 12″ each)

Plate 37
Daitoku-ji Temple by Kiyoshi Saito
The wood grain is utilized in the background, and you will probably notice it is seasoned. The lines were carved with a knife for the most part. The ink was not applied so heavily and the printing is strong and clear.
(Size: 98" × 114")

Plate 38
Beach at Low Tide by Fumio Kitaoka
All the lines were carved with a knife. Accordingly,
the picture has a clean, clear appearance.
(Size: 140″×216″)

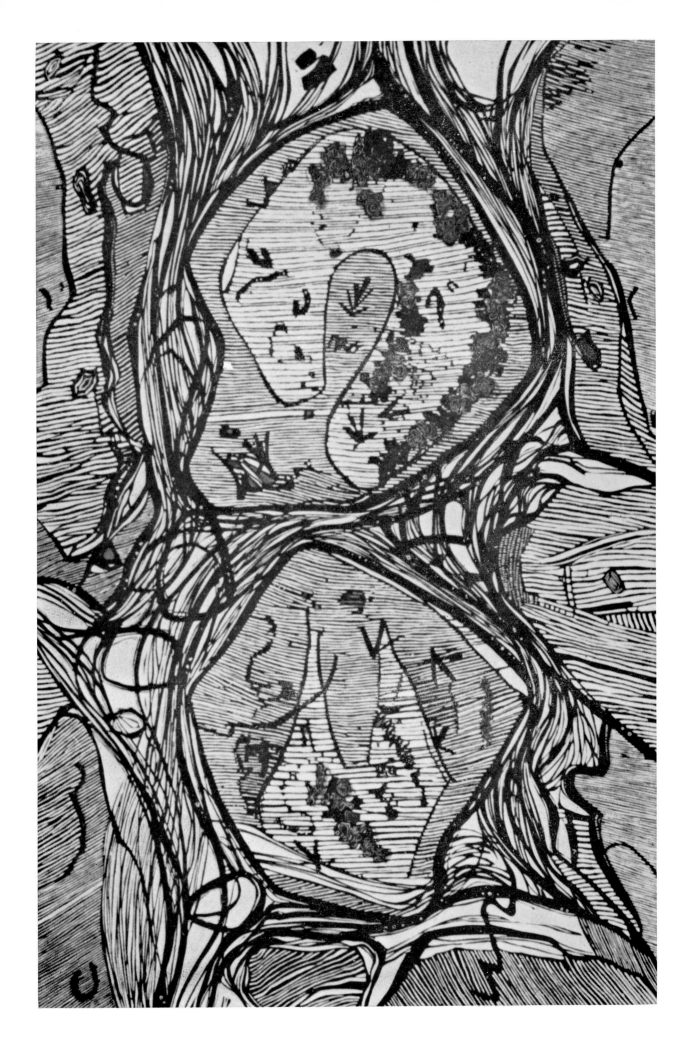

Plate 39
Roadside Deity by Hodaka Yoshida
The knife, gouge, veiner, and other chisels were used to carve this. A little ink and much pressure in printing were used to produce the feeling of clarity. (Size: 34″ × 110″)

Plate 40

Falling Leaves by Hideo Hagiwara

This composition had the various effects of methods of printing as its aim. The appearance of the black spots on the surface and the feeling of complexity was produced by printing the back using light pressure which resulted in blotting through to the front. (Size: 49″×90″)

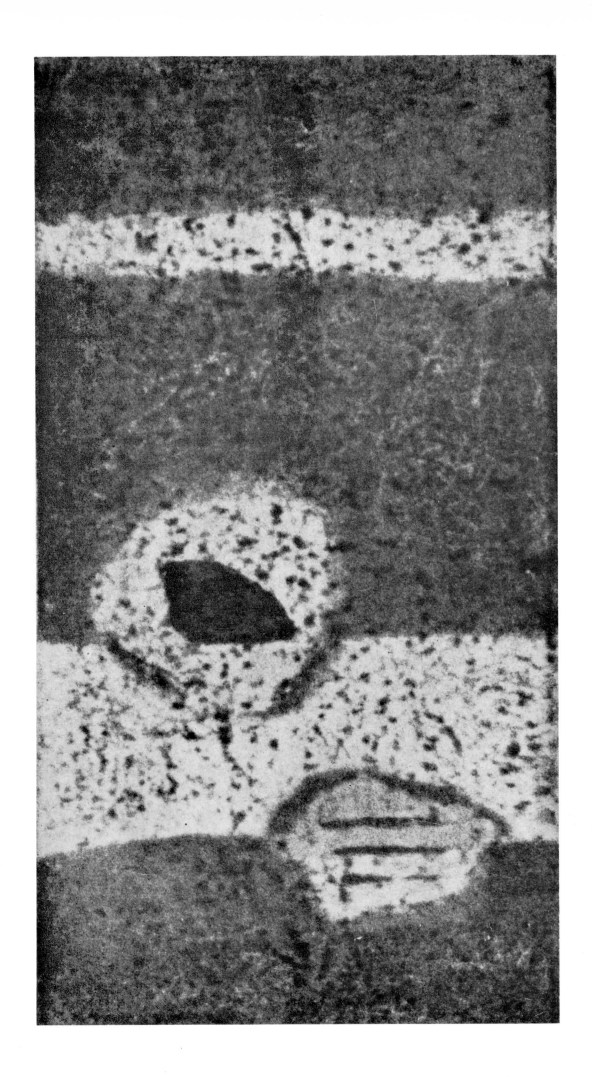

Plate 41

Meeting by Takumi Shinagawa

A special material was applied to the block to give the face a texture different from wood, then inked and printed. This is what gives it a rough appearance. Plastic paints and other materials are often used in cases like this.

(Size: 94′×131″)

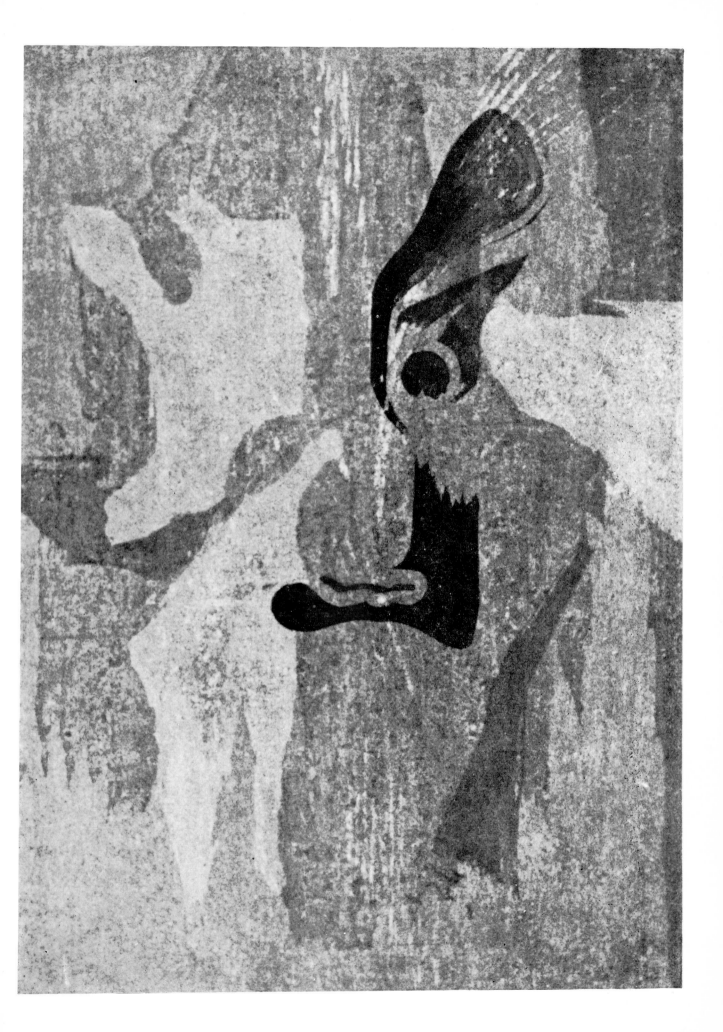

Prints for Christmas Cards

The small prints shown in Color Plates 9-12 are actual
size.   They are examples of works which can be used
for Christmas cards or similar purposes.

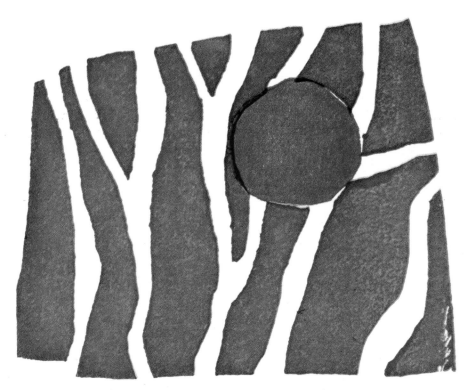

Color Plate 9   The Sun and Trees, by a school-boy

Color Plate 10   Himeji Castle, by Oki-ie Hashimoto

Color Plate 11   Lullaby, by Toru Mabuchi

Color Plate 12   Cat, by Tomo-o Inagaki

INVENTORY 1983